Can Science Solve?

The Mystery of Crop Circles

Chris Oxlade

Heinemann Library
Chicago, Illinois

© 1999 Reed Educational and Professional Publishing
Published by Heinemann Library,
an imprint of Reed Educational & Professional Publishing,
Chicago, IL

Customer Service 888-454-2279

Visit our website at www.heinemannlibrary.com

Designed by AMR Ltd.

Cover photograph reproduced with permission of Fortean Picture Library.
Printed in China

05
10 9 8 7

Library of Congress Cataloging-in-Publication Data

Oxlade, Chris
        The mystery of crop circles / Chris Oxlade.
            p. cm.— (Can science solve?)
        Includes bibliographical references.
        Summary: Describes the appearance of the phenomena know as crop circles and offers various explanations as to how they were created.
        ISBN 1-57572-804-4 (lib. bdg.)   ISBN 1-58810-308-0 (pbk. bdg.)
        1. Science--Miscellanea--Juvenile literature. 2. Crop circles---Miscellanea--Juvenile literature.   3. Curiosities and wonders--Miscellanea--Juvenile literature.   [1. Crop circles.] I. Title.
        II. Series.
Q173.092   1999
001.944.—dc21   98-54489
                                                                                                    CIP
                                                                                                    AC

Acknowledgements

The Publishers would like to thank the following for permission to reproduce photographs: Fortean Picture Library, pp. 6, 9, 13, 14, 29; Alberta UFO Study Group, p. 5; P. Broadhurst, p. 15; W. Burger, p. 23; Dr. G. T. Meaden, p.10; E .Ross, p.18; F. Taylor, pp. 7, 25, 28; TORRO, p. 20; Oxford Scientific Films/W. Faidley, p. 21; Punch Limited, p. 26; Science Photo Library/P. Menzel, p. 22; Still Pictures/T. Thomas p.17.

Every effort has been made to contact copyright holders of any material reproduced in this book. Any omissions will be rectified in subsequent printings if notice is given to the Publisher.

Some words are shown in bold, **like this**. You can find out what they mean by looking in the glossary.

Contents

Unsolved Mysteries 4

The Circles Appear 6

Did You See That? 8

Physical Evidence....................10

Circle Formations....................12

Evidence on the Ground 14

The Theories 16

The UFO Theory....................18

Earth and Sky Theories 20

Whirlwinds and Plasma....................22

Famous Fakes....................24

Why Fake Crop Circles?.....................26

In Conclusion 28

Glossary....................*30*

More Books to Read....................*31*

Index *32*

Unsolved Mysteries

For centuries, people have been puzzled and fascinated by mysterious creatures, places, and events. Is there really a monster living in Loch Ness? Did the lost city of Atlantis ever exist? Are UFOs actually vehicles from outer space? Who is responsible for the strange patterns called crop circles—clever hoaxers or alien beings? Some of these mysteries even baffle scientists. Many scientists have spent years trying to find the answer. But just how far can science go? Can it really explain the seemingly unexplainable? Are there some mysteries that science simply cannot solve? Read on, and make up your own mind.

This book tells you about the history of crop circles. You'll read about eyewitness accounts, scientific evidence found at crop circles, and different theories to explain how they form.

What is a crop circle?

You may have seen pictures of crop circles. They are circular patterns that mysteriously appear in crop fields. Inside the circle, the crop stalks are bent over, but at the edge, the crops are untouched. Circles last until the crop is harvested. Crop circles are not always one, perfect circle. Often, two or more crop circles appear in the same field. Some circles are oval-shaped. Others are complex designs. Crop circle researchers call these **pictograms**.

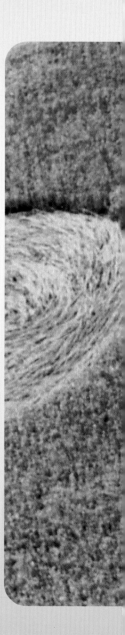

Crop circles first made the news in the early 1980s. At that time, dozens popped up around the world. Media coverage was high because UFO enthusiasts claimed that the circles were made by aliens. Crop circles are so neat that they look artificial. In fact, most turn out to be hoaxes. But, there are many that cannot be explained. Is there anything science can do to solve the mystery?

This set of crop circles, found in Alberta, Canada, in 1991, shows the typical spiral pattern of the bent crop stalks inside a circle.

The Circles Appear

Headlines about crop circles first appeared in newspapers and on television in the early 1980s. But this was not the first time crop circles had been seen. There had been several reports from Australia, the United States, Canada, and England in the 1960s and 1970s. Only a few were reported earlier. The earliest record of a crop circle is from Holland in 1590. Many farmers had seen crop circles before, but they thought the wind had formed them.

A crop of circles

During the early 1980s, reports of crop circles rose dramatically. Dozens of circles appeared each summer. Most were in the English **counties** of Hampshire and Wiltshire. Many were near the town of Warminster, also famous for UFO sightings. For a few years, crop circles received huge media coverage. At the same time, the film *E.T.: The Extraterrestrial* came out. It was about an alien left on Earth after its spaceship took off. The film caused more people to think about aliens coming to Earth. By the late 1980s, reports of crop circles were coming in from all over the world. In 1990, more than a thousand circles were reported.

An engraving from 1678 appears to show a crop circle. The report with the engraving says that the circle was made overnight by the "mowing devil."

The Mowing - Devil :

Or, Strange *NEWS* out of

Hartford - fhire.

Being a True Relation of a Farmer, who Bargaining with a Poor Mower, about the Cutting down Three Half Acres of Oats; upon the Mower's asking too much, the Farmer fwore, That the Devil fhould Mow it, rather than He. And fo it fell out, that that very Night, the Crop of Oat fhew'd as if it had been all of a Flame; but next Morning appear'd fo neatly Mow'd by the Devil, or fome Infernal Spirit, that no Mortal Man was able to do the like. Alfo, How the faid Oats ly now in the Field, and the Owner has not Power to fetch them away.

Modern patterns

Crop circles still appear today. But something about them has changed. In the 1990s, the designs became more complex. People were finding crop circles that were squares, triangles, mathematical patterns, and letters. Researchers call these complicated crop circle patterns **agriglyphs**.

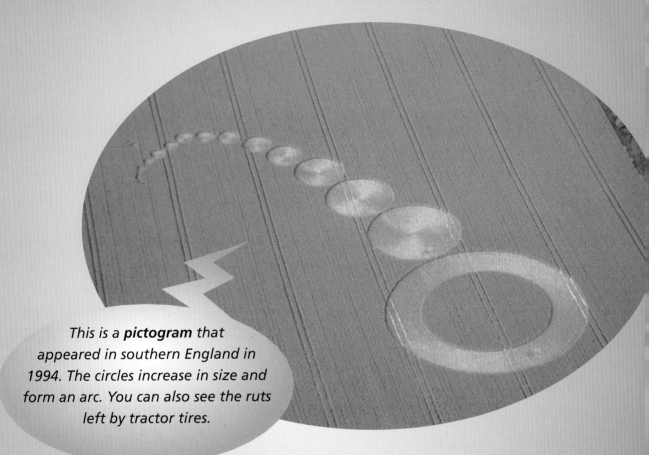

*This is a **pictogram** that appeared in southern England in 1994. The circles increase in size and form an arc. You can also see the ruts left by tractor tires.*

Circles around the world

Most crop circle reports come from southern England. But crop circles show up all over the world. They are found on every continent and in more than 70 countries, including the United States, Canada, Australia, Japan, France, and India. Crop circles have also been found in different types of fields, from tobacco to rice. Circle formations have also been found in sand and snow.

Did You See That?

The thousands of crop circles that have turned up in the last 30 years only appear in certain places. Many people have seen and photographed the existing crop circles. But very few people have witnessed them being made. Could this be because most crop circles form in the night?

Queensland, Australia, January 1966

George Pedley was driving his tractor through a field of sugarcane when he saw what he described as a blue-grey spaceship fly out of a swamp. It dove, rose, and flew off, spinning all the time. In the reeds where he had seen the spaceship rise, Pedley found a 99 foot- (30 meter-) wide circle. He described the reeds as having been "subjected to some terrific **rotary** force." The reeds look as though they'd been twirled around. Nearby, he found two more circles that looked like they had been made in the same way.

Wiltshire, England, August 1983

Melvyn Bell was riding his horse on the hills of the northern edge of Salisbury Plain in southern England. A whirlwind of dust **spiralling** up from a wheat field caught his eye. It was about 165 feet (50 meters) away. In a few seconds, before his eyes, a crop circle formed. When it was over, dust and a few broken stalks fell from the air around the edge of the circle.

Hambledon, England, August 1990

Gary and Vivienne Tomlinson were walking through a corn field late one evening. The corn swayed in the breeze. As they watched, they noticed a disturbance in the middle of the field. Then they heard a whistle. They said, "a large whirlwind" began to push the corn down. Smaller whirlwinds also began appearing and disappearing. "We stood watching in amazement, the corn swirled and then laid down."

Lights in the sky, like this one, are sometimes seen at the same time as crop circles are formed. This light appeared in New Jersey. It is called the "spook light."

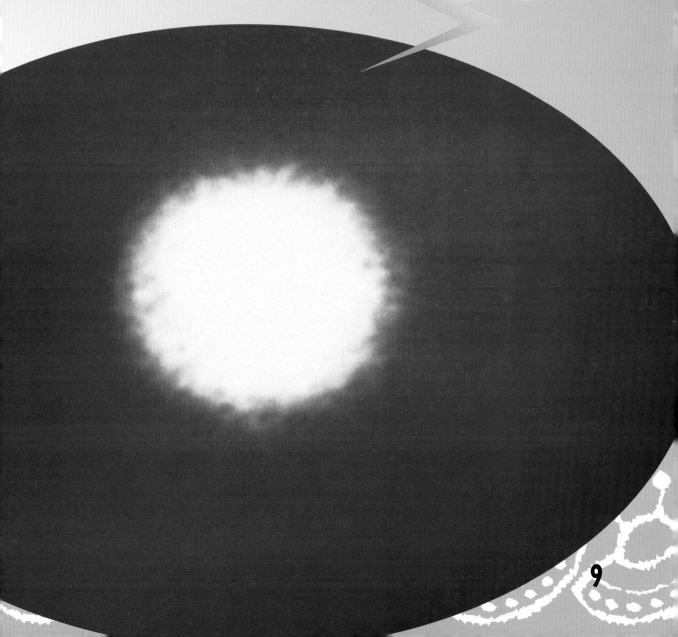

Physical Evidence

What do crop circles really look like? What scientific evidence does a crop circle researcher look for at a crop circle site?

The size of the circles varies widely. They measure from about 3 feet (1 meter) to 165 feet (50 meters) across. **Pictograms** and crop circles in complex patterns are much larger. They are rarely perfect circles. Most are lightly stretched circles, called ellipses. The swirling pattern does not always start in the exact center of the crop circle.

Here, British crop circle researcher Dr. Terence Meaden is measuring a circle formed in Wiltshire, England, in 1991.

Edges and swirls

Two of the most noticeable features of a crop circle are the well-defined edge and the **spiral** pattern of the flattened stalks. The edge looks finely cut. The stalks inside the circle are flattened. Those that make up the edge are left standing.

In a crop circle, the stalks are bent into a "swirl pattern." This is usually a spiral. The stalks in the center point toward the outside. The stalks at the edge point along the **circumference**. Sometimes there are two spiral centers. Some spirals circle clockwise. Others circle counterclockwise. Patterns that have more than one circle may spiral in both directions.

If you look closely at the swirl patterns, you will see they are not as simple as they seem. If there is more than one layer, the top layer may swirl clockwise and the bottom layer may circle counterclockwise.

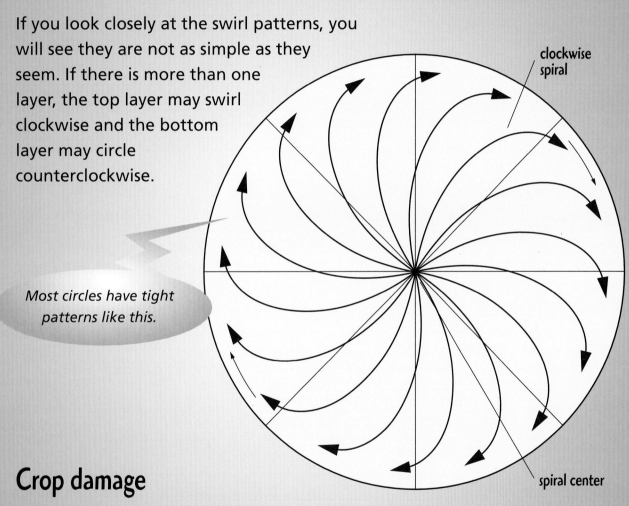

clockwise spiral

spiral center

Most circles have tight patterns like this.

Crop damage

Surprisingly, most crop stalks inside the crop circle are not broken. They are just bent over. The crop is unharmed. It will even keep growing as if nothing has happened.

Circle Formations

Crop circles are rarely perfect circles. Often, they are not single, or simple, circles at all. Crop circles can form in groups. They can be surrounded by thin crop rings. Some have lines leading away from them. Others are not even circular. **Pictograms** or **agriglyphs** are highly designed crop circles.

Basic formations

The most simple crop circle formation is the single circle. They can come in pairs (doublets). There are even groups of three (triplets) and four (quadruplets). Some crop circles have one or two thin rings around them. These rings may be only a few inches wide.

A quintuplet formation is the shape of a cross. It consists of a single circle with four smaller "satellite" circles around it. The size of the circles, the thickness of the rings, and the distances between the circles can vary.

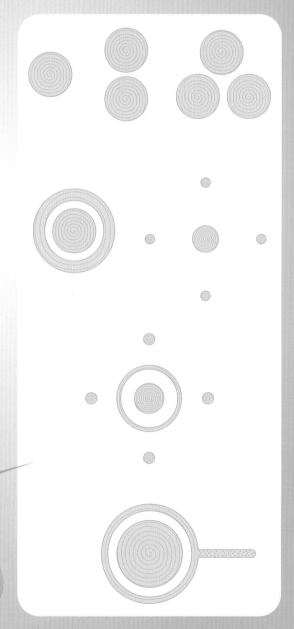

These are the basic forms of crop circles found so far. The single circle is the most common.

Spurs and ruts

Some crop circles have a line of flattened crops, called a spur, leading away from them. The spurs often follow the ruts formed by tractor tires. Fake crop circles can be made without damaging the crops by walking in the tire ruts.

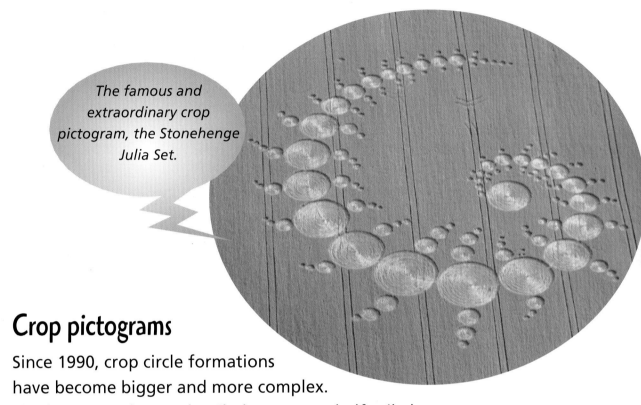

The famous and extraordinary crop pictogram, the Stonehenge Julia Set.

Crop pictograms

Since 1990, crop circle formations have become bigger and more complex. The largest and most detailed are over a half-mile long (1 kilometer). These are the pictograms or agriglyphs. They make up one-fourth of the crop circles.

Some formations are based on complex mathematical patterns. One such formation appeared on July 7, 1990. It was found at Stonehenge, in Wiltshire, England. It was 990 feet (300 meters) across. It was made of 149 separate circles and formed the Julia Set, a mathematical pattern. The Julia Set is similar to **fractal patterns** drawn by computers.

Evidence on the Ground

You've read about the different sizes, shapes, and patterns made by the crop stalks inside the circles. But what other evidence can be found at crop circle sites? Clues can be found on the ground or in the crops.

The lay of the land

Most, but not all, crop circles appear in fields near the bottom of small, steep hills. Crop circle researchers look for clues in the direction the hillside faces. They also look at the direction of the prevailing wind—the way the wind blows most often. They look at these conditions because most crop circles form when the wind blows over the hill toward the field.

This is the gentle, rolling countryside of Wiltshire, England. Many crop circles form at the bases of these hills.

Energy fields

Researchers have tested the area inside crop circles for **electromagnetic radiation** and **magnetic fields**. Some circles do send out weak radiation. Radiation may be present for several days after the crop circle has appeared. Magnetic fields much stronger than the earth's magnetic field have also been detected. Reports of compasses spinning out of control and electrical equipment failing inside crop circles have been recorded.

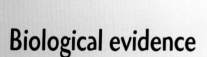

Hamish Miller is using a **divining** rod to locate clues from underground. Perhaps some feature of the earth causes crop circles to form.

Biological evidence

The respected American **biophysicist** Dr. William Levengood has conducted tests on wheat stalks in and around crop circles. He found that the bumps, or nodes, on the stalks in the crop circles were larger than those outside of it. He thinks microwave heating may be the cause. He thinks the same kind of heat that microwave ovens use to cook food may do something to create crop circles. Another interesting finding is that the bent crops inside crop circles actually grow better than those outside.

The Theories

Many people have many different theories about what causes crop circles. Some theories are carefully thought out. Researchers interview eyewitnesses and take samples from the crop circles. Other theories are based on ideas that cannot be tested scientifically. One theory suggests that animals make crop circles during courtship.

Why is it so difficult to solve the riddle of crop circles in a scientific way? Researchers have not been able to observe crop circles forming. No one can predict where or when a crop circle will form next. Therefore, no one can plan where, when, or how to set up an investigation. One theory states that all crop circles are fakes. Many fakes have been uncovered. Another theory is that they are linked to UFOs.

Here are some other theories:

Underground patterns

Some theories say that crop circles are caused by things underground or in the soil. Researchers are trying to figure out if decay from ancient crops or buildings left something in the soil. They are looking into bombs that exploded during World War Two. Could something in the soil or deep underground cause crop circles?

You can see the circular pattern of wind created by this helicopter's rotor, but could it cause a crop circle?

Aircraft

Could helicopters make crop circles? One of the first theories tried to prove that helicopter **downdraft** created them. But researchers found that downdraft could not form the **spiral** or the neat edges. Another theory was that the wingtips of aircraft created swirls of air that caused crop circles to form. But this was disproved when researchers couldn't locate any crop circles below common flight paths.

Atmospheric effects

The most scientific theories say that crop circles are created naturally by spinning air. Do you think a crop circle could be formed by a tornado or another form of moving air?

The UFO Theory

The most popular theory about crop circle formation is that the circles and **pictograms** are made by an alien lifeform. Supporters of the "UFO theory" think that the circles may be produced when an alien spacecraft lands or takes off. They also suggest that the aliens make the crop circles to try to communicate with us. Some researchers have tried to **decipher** the more complex crop circle shapes by comparing them to ancient forms of writing, such as **hieroglyphics**.

This photo shows bright lights photographed in 1995 over the island of Madeira, in the Atlantic Ocean. Similar lights have been seen near new crop circles.

For and against

There are a few pieces of evidence to support the UFO theory. For example, several eyewitnesses report strange lights moving in the sky the night before a fresh crop circle is discovered in that area. And the most complex pictograms, if they are not hoaxes, are impossible to explain by any other theory.

As you might expect, there are strong arguments against the UFO theory. For example, if highly intelligent aliens are trying to communicate with us, why wouldn't they do it so we could understand? Arguments against the landing site theory ask some interesting questions. Why would the crops be swirled but otherwise undamaged? And why do the sites keep changing size and shape?

The UFO theory is interesting because it's related to science fiction and the unknown. But it relies on belief rather than scientific proof. Of course, as of now, the theory is impossible to disprove.

Study groups

There are several organizations that research and study crop circles. Some of their members approach the subject from a scientific point of view. Some, who call themselves cereologists, look at crop circles from a mystical point of view. Among them are the Center for Crop Circle Studies (CCCS), the Circles Effect Research Unit (CERES), and Circles Phenomenon Research (CPR). There are several interesting crop circle web sites on the Internet. You can find them using the search term crop circles.

Earth and Sky Theories

Along with the UFO theory is the "earth energy" theory. This says that crop circles are somehow created by the earth itself. They state that the earth is sending a message to stop pollution and habitat destruction. This theory is related to James Lovelock's **Gaia hypothesis**. The Gaia hypothesis states that the earth acts like a living being. The theory is supported by some mystics, **paranormalists,** and **ecologists**.

The theory also ties in with other facts about crop circles. Many crop circles appear near UFO "hotspots." Supporters of the theory also link the circles to **ley lines**. These ancient lines are thought to be "energy paths" on the earth's surface.

Swirling winds

The most scientific theory is that crop circles are created by some sort of swirling air current, called a **vortex**. Different kinds of vortices occur naturally in the atmosphere. Examples of vortices are tornadoes and whirlwinds. There is evidence to support this theory. The stalks in the crop circle seem to have been swirled by a flow of air. And several eyewitness reports talk about swirling winds and dust.

This photo shows a fast-spinning tornado vortex reaching down from storm clouds to the ground.

There is another argument that leads scientists to think that crop circles are linked to the weather. Crop circles normally appear during the summer. They form in the late evening or early morning when the air is often still and warm.

This is tornado damage in Texas—far worse and over a larger area than seen at crop circle sites.

Tornadoes

Could crop circles be formed by tornadoes? Tornadoes do swirl and pick up things from the ground. But there are several reasons why tornadoes cannot be responsible. First, tornadoes only form from enormous thunderclouds. This type of weather condition is not mentioned in eyewitness reports. Second, tornadoes normally cause much more damage than is seen in crop circles.

Whirlwinds and Plasma

A whirlwind is a small **vortex** of air. Whirlwinds are much smaller than tornadoes. They do not form in thunderclouds like tornadoes. They rise up from warm ground on hot, still days. Whirlwinds often lift dust from the ground. That is why they are also called "dust devils." Whirlwinds usually don't stay in one place. Sometimes they move. Small vortices are often formed when wind blows over the edge of a hill. You can see similar **eddies** spinning dust and leaves when the wind blows past the corner of a building.

The Plasma Vortex Theory

Dr. Terence Meaden is a leading expert on tornadoes and whirlwinds. He is the head of the Tornado and Storm Research Organization (TORRO), based in Wiltshire, England. In the 1980s, he developed the theory that whirlwinds and eddies are responsible for crop circles. But not ordinary whirlwinds and eddies. Only the ones in which the air is **electrically charged**. The charged air is called **plasma**. The theory is known as the "Plasma Vortex Theory." Plasma vortices form from whirlwinds and eddies. They can stay in the air for several minutes before touching the ground to make crop circles.

This globe is filled with low-pressure gas. The gas becomes plasma when electricity is supplied to the globe. Touching the globe makes the plasma turn back to gas in some places, giving off a strange glow.

Light and sound

The magnetic fields and electrical currents caused by spinning plasma can create humming sounds and light. These fields could explain equipment failures inside crop circles and the biological changes in the crops. They can even explain the strange sensations some eyewitnesses report, such as their hair standing on end. Glowing lights and humming sounds are often been reported by eyewitnesses. Also, a plasma vortex naturally moves as if it is under remote control. However, it can remain in one place for minutes .The way a plasma vortex looks and moves may be mistaken for a UFO.

Could this photograph show ball lightning? Ball lightning is an uncommon type of lightning. It may act like a plasma vortex.

Famous Fakes

There are more faked crop circles than all other mysterious happenings put together. It's likely that more than nine out of ten crop circles are hoaxes. Here you can find out about some famous hoaxes.

Doug and Dave

The most famous crop circle hoaxers of all time are two British artists. Doug Bower and Dave Chorley are known in crop circle studies as "Doug and Dave." In September 1991, Doug and Dave claimed that they had faked more than 200 crop circles since 1978, including many that were thought to be real. Doug and Dave also said that they knew several other people who fake crop circles. Some "experts" responded by saying that they already knew many circles were fake, but that they also knew of some that were real.

Faking a crop circle

A convincing crop circle can be made by walking in ever-increasing circles, tamping down the crop. By walking along the existing tire ruts, hoaxers can get to the crop circle site without leaving a trail in the field.

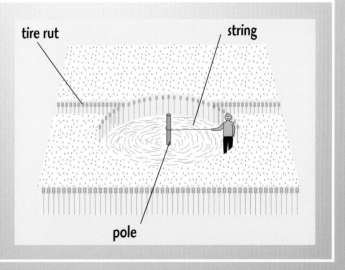

tire rut

string

pole

Here, crop circle faker Jim Schnabel is at work in a field in southern England in 1993.

More hoaxers

Rob Irving of Great Britain and an American, Jim Schnabel, are crop circle hoaxers. In the summers of 1992 and 1993, they wanted to show how easy it is to fake crop circles. Two other hoaxers, John Lundburg and Rod Dickenson, also fake circles, but they are not trying to fool people. They call themselves crop artists. Dickenson says he knows who faked the incredible Stonehenge Julia Set and how it was done.

Media hoaxes

Television and newspaper reporters have faked crop circles. They wanted to see if they could fool crop circle experts. In 1991, a British television company faked a crop circle. They asked an "Earth energy" believer and Dr. Terence Meaden to look at it. Both experts thought that it was real. The British newspaper, *Today,* also tricked an expert. One of the leading UFOlogists, Pat Delgado, once described a crop circle by Doug and Dave as something "no human" could have made.

Why Fake Crop Circles?

We know that most crop circles are fakes. But why do people make crop circles? What is the point?

Some hoaxers fake circles for fun. Perhaps others do it on a dare. There are many stories of agricultural students making circles as a prank. In the 1990s, several hoaxers who make **pictograms** started to call themselves crop artists. They believe they are guided by some **paranormal** force. They say that the fields are the canvas and the crops are the paints.

The most famous hoaxers have created some crop circles simply to test the knowledge of crop circle researchers.

This cartoon from Punch *magazine makes fun of the crop circle **phenomenon**. This crop circle seems to have been made by a shopping cart.*

Is it all a hoax?

Some people claim that the whole crop circle phenomenon is a huge hoax. They claim that all crop circles are fake. Researchers, whether they believe that the crop circles are caused by weather conditions or made by aliens, admit that most circles are fake. But they are sure that some are real. There are several arguments in their favor. It is very unlikely that all the crop circles around the world could have been faked. Some circles are found away from tire ruts and no paths lead to them. Also, there were reports of crop circles made hundreds of years ago. Eyewitnesses claim to have seen them being made. Many crop circles show up near major roads. It is unlikely that hoaxers could have faked those without getting caught, even at night.

In Conclusion

Can science really solve the mystery of crop circles? The lack of solid and reliable scientific evidence means this question cannot be answered at this time. Dozens of researchers have studied crop circles closely, and still there is no conclusive evidence about where they come from and how they are made. Many different theories are being examined. Many theories have already been disproved. There are some scientific theories that are still being investigated.

Is plasma the answer?

The **Plasma Vortex** Theory seems to explain the formation of most crop circles. It does match with what eyewitnesses have seen. Japanese scientists have been able to create small plasma vortices in the laboratory. But the physics of plasma is quite a new science. It is not really understood yet. Although these experiments prove that plasma vortices exist, they do not prove that they are responsible for crop circles. The main argument against the theory is that it cannot explain the **pictogram** crop circles. Supporters of the theory believe that all pictograms are hoaxes.

This is a crop circle pictogram formed in southern England in 1995. The plasma theory cannot explain this. Do you think it looks real or like it's a hoax?

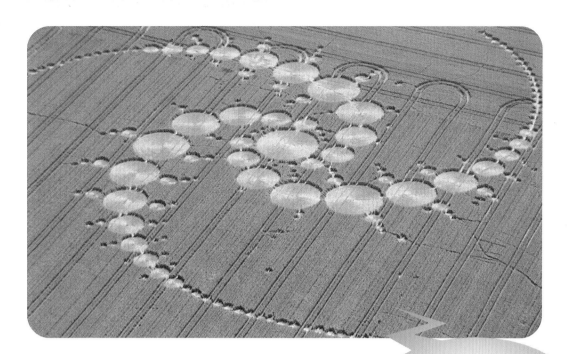

What do you think?

You have read about crop circles and the possible explanations for them. Can you draw any conclusions? Do you feel that you can dismiss any of the theories without investigating them further? Do you have any theories of your own?

This photo shows a remarkable crop circle pictogram formed in Wiltshire, England.

What about the UFO theory, or the Earth Energy Theory? Can you rule either one out? Perhaps one is the answer and we don't have the scientific understanding yet. Do you believe that every crop circle is a hoax? Can you support the Plasma Vortex Theory before it has been proved or disproved?

Try to keep an open mind. Remember that if scientists throughout history had not investigated everything that appeared to be strange or mysterious, many scientific discoveries may never have been made.

Glossary

agriglyph complex shape or form of flattened crops

biophysics branch of science that uses physics to help study biology

circumference distance around the outside edge of a circle

county administrative area of the United Kingdom

decipher to figure out the hidden message in a code of words or pictures

divining finding water or underground objects using intuition or guesswork, often using two rods that swing across each other when water or an object is near

downdraft air current that blows vertically downward

ecologist scientist who studies the relationship between living things and their environments

eddy circular movement of air causing a small whirlwind

electrical charge build up or deficit of electrons—the tiny particles that are part of an atom

electromagnetic radiation rays or waves that are part of the electromagnetic spectrum, including light rays, radio waves, microwaves, X-rays, and nuclear radiation

fractal pattern mathematical pattern made by repeating the same simple pattern again and again, but moving, rotating, and changing its size each time

Gaia hypothesis theory that states that all the plants and animals on Earth, together with the seas and atmosphere, act as a huge organism that can change the earth's environment

hieroglyphics form of writing that uses pictures instead of letters

ley lines straight lines across the landscape made by ancient tracks or linking ancient monuments–thought by some people to be ancient roads–and by others to be lines of mysterious energy

magnetic field area around a magnet where its magnetic effect can be felt

paranormal anything that cannot be explained by scientific investigation

phenomenon remarkable or unexplained happening

pictogram picture or symbol that represents a word or a phrase

plasma air that has become electrically charged

rotary spinning around a center point

spiral shape that gets smaller as it moves around a center point

vortex rotating mass of air or water (more than one are vortices)

More Books to Read

Innes, Brian. *Alien Visitors and Abductions.* Austin, Tex.: Raintree Steck-Vaughn Publishers, 1999.

Innes, Brian. *Mysteries of the Ancients.* Austin, Tex.: Raintree Steck-Vaughn Publishers, 1999.

Index

aliens 18, 19

Australia 6, 7, 8

ball lightning 23

Bell, Melvyn 8

Canada 5, 6, 7

crop circles

    appearance of 4, 10, 11

    effect on crops 11, 15

    study groups 19

    types of 7, 12

Dickenson, Rod 25

divining 15

Doug and Dave 24, 25

dust devils 22

E.T.: The Extraterrestrial 6

Gaia hypothesis 20

helicopters 17

hieroglyphics 18

hoaxes 5, 24, 25, 26, 27, 28

Holland 6

Julia Set 13, 25

Levengood, Dr. William 15

ley lines 20

Lundburg, John 25

magnetic field 15, 23

Meaden, Dr. Terence 11, 22, 25

Pedley, George 8

Plasma Vortex Theory 22, 28

Punch magazine 26

Schnabel, Jim 25

Stonehenge 13, 25

Tomlinson, Gary and Vivienne 9

tornado *see* whirlwind

UFOs 5, 6, 16, 18, 19, 20, 23, 29

United Kingdom 6, 7, 8, 9

United States 6, 7

Warminster, England 6

whirlwind 8, 9, 17, 20, 21, 22